Imtiaz Dharker

I SPEAK FOR
THE DEVIL

BLOODAXE BOOKS

ISBN: 1 85224 569 7

First published 2001 by
Bloodaxe Books Ltd,
Highgreen,
Tarset,
Northumberland NE48 1RP.

Bloodaxe Books Ltd acknowledges
the financial assistance of Northern Arts.

Cover printing by J. Thomson Colour Printers Ltd, Glasgow.

Printed in Great Britain by
Cromwell Press Ltd, Trowbridge, Wiltshire.

For all the ones
who stood up
and spoke out.
For the ones
who are still struggling
to find their feet
and their voices.

For the ones
who have nothing left
to be afraid of.
For all the others
who haven't yet begun.

For you,
in hope...

ACKNOWLEDGEMENTS

'They'll say, "She must be from another country" ' was broadcast on *Open Minds* (BBC 2 Television) and on Outlook (BBC Radio). 'At the Lahore Karhai' was first published in *Mosaic* (Penguin Books, India, 1999) and 'The Orders' and 'Stitched' in *Stand*. Some of the drawings in this book are owned by the following people and companies, and the author and publishers would like to acknowledge their kind support: Nira and Shyam Benegal; Monika and Charles Correa; Uma and Gerson da Cunha; Mala and Harsh Goenka; Sugandha and Jai Hiremath; Chitra and Ashok Hiremath; Ajoy Kapoor; Sheena and Kunal Kapoor; Tasneem and Vikram Mehta; Ismail Merchant; Laxmi Nair, Gallerie Leela; Mr and Mrs Subramaniam; Samir Somiya; Susi and Aart Weijburg.

CONTENTS

THEY'LL SAY, 'SHE MUST BE FROM ANOTHER COUNTRY'

13 Honour killing
14 The orders
16 Here
17 There
18 Stitched
20 Announcing the departure...
22 Tongue
24 12 noon
25 Crab-apples
26 Front door
27 Announcing the arrival...
28 Monsoon words
31 Announcing the arrival...
32 At the Lahore Karhai
36 Hanging Gardens
37 Not a muslim burial
38 They'll say, 'She must be from another country'

THE BROKEN UMBRELLA

43 The umbrella
44 Outside
45 Keeping guard
46 In a cold place
47 Today we spoke
48 Dot
50 Knees
51 Sofa
52 Chair
53 Yellow today

I SPEAK FOR THE DEVIL

57 The djinn in Auntie
60 All of us
62 Power
64 Breeding ground, Chicago
66 Learning to speak in Birmingham
68 Being good in Glasgow

69 Chilli-hot
70 'Have you ever lost control?'
72 Lines of control
73 The eyelid trembles
74 The location
75 In
76 Close-circuit
77 The devil's day
79 In bed with the devil
80 Saviours
83 The devil to the poet
85 Slit
86 Mobile
87 This room
88 Guardians
91 In your face
92 Ceilings
93 Mischief-maker
94 Remote control
95 Dealing with the devil
96 Bai settles down
97 It brings the battle into your living-room
97 The devil to god
98 Greater glory
99 Secrets
101 A short detour from dying
102 Canvas
105 Compromising positions
108 Object
111 Medlar
112 Possession
115 The devil's advice
116 Prayer in the park
117 Blackbox
118 Undressing
119 The devil's valentine
119 Yes, I drank the wine
120 Squatter: left shoulder
121 Last House-Full Show
127 Exorcism

**They'll say,
'She must be
from another country'**

In Lahore, in the last year of the
20th century, a woman was shot
by her family in her lawyer's office.
Her crime was that she had asked
for a divorce.
The whole Pakistan Senate refused
to condemn the act.
They called it an 'honour killing'.

Honour killing

At last I'm taking off this coat,
    this black coat of a country
    that I swore for years was mine,
    that I wore more out of habit
    than design.
    Born wearing it,
    I believed I had no choice.

I'm taking off this veil,
    this black veil of a faith
    that made me faithless
    to myself,
    that tied my mouth,
    gave my god a devil's face,
    and muffled my own voice.

I'm taking off these silks,
    these lacy things
    that feed dictator dreams,
    the mangalsutra and the rings
    rattling in a tin cup of needs
    that beggared me.

I'm taking off this skin,
    and then the face, the flesh,
    the womb.

Let's see
    what I am in here
    when I squeeze past
    the easy cage of bone.

Let's see
    what I am out here,
    making, crafting,
    plotting
    at my new geography.

The orders

Someone else gives the orders here.
The carcass is lying on the boat.
I remember seeing this
with my enemy's eyes.

I'm wandering on all fours
between the rows of cars
There's my reflection in the chrome,
my matted fur.
There's your skin, stretched
across the window-pane.
The light is slanting in.

Is this a house?
There is a number on the door,
but no name.

Why is this mirror broken?
It makes sense of my disordered face.

I'll go.
I must have stayed too long.
I've begun to look like you.

Is that my shoe
floating on the water?

Here

There are too many people
in this room.

Outside, the landscape turns
from trees to urgent arms,
hands, fingers, blossoming fingernails.

Faces burn
their way out of the sides of hills.

Thousands of people moved
from here to there.
Their feet left trails
that shifted with the wind.

Worse than leaving a country
is walking out of a door
that will stand open
because you have told all
your secrets, and there is nothing
left to steal.

In another place,
people begin to shout.
The top comes off my head.
All the light flies out.

Whether I stand on this side
of the borderline, or that,
the colour keeps sliding
off my face.

There

The house just grew
without a plan, rooms
and stairwells added on
as the need arose,
not a place an architect
would choose to build.

Things happened. Walls came up,
a door punched through.
You decided where to place a step,
a window-frame,
here a table, there a chair.

You filled the house with children,
sofas, servants, every space occupied,
but the walls were always bare.

That was your choice,
remote in your decisions,
the master of the house.
When you came home,
we crept around you quietly,
massaged your feet.

I left one day.
You never wrote.

Twenty years late, I came back.
The children and the sofa sets had gone.
You sat there with the television on;
a fax machine, a phone.

But on every inch of space on every wall,
in room after room,
you had framed and hung
every childish line that I had ever drawn.

Now it doesn't matter when I speak.
It will always be too late.

Stitched

Someone stitched on my head and hands
but they used some foreign stuff
that pointed out the parts
where I'd been mended.

And so my mouth spoke Punjabi
while my brain heard Scots.
My ears followed German
and my tongue did French.
It seems they were about to put me out
in a garbage bag, I looked so odd.

But I survived,
and they got used to the way I was.
Sometimes they act as if
I'm one of them.

I'm not always sure I did the right thing.
Maybe it's time to do dangerous somersaults,
to jump and dance and run.
Maybe it's time, again, to come undone.

Announcing the departure...

There's safety in a ticket:
the option of setting off.
In my mind my bags
are always packed,
zipped and labelled,
locked and tagged.

But every plane or train I catch
just brings me back
into this waiting space.
Glasgow, Baroda, Sialkot, Rome.
The names are roads of possibilities
that turn into lanes
with the undertow of home.
Every new city, every street
I get to pulls the ground away
from underneath my feet.

I think my body is asking
to be in some promised place.
I think my body is begging
for another face.

Yesterday I put my name
inside a parcel, and sent it off
by courier, marked 'Urgent'
to some address

unknown.

Tongue

'Your tongue is fighting me.'
This sounds familiar, but
the source is new.
Dr Naterwala, one of the kindest
dentists I have met,
struggling with a back tooth
and twenty years of trauma,
has decided that
enough is enough.

'Your tongue must learn to keep still.'
This I've heard often,
but not in such a literal sense.
Keeping my tongue still,
all of my life,
has been a highly recommended skill.

'I want to help you.
Just forget your tongue.'
Oh Dr Naterwala,
you'd be amused if you knew
how often I'd been accused
of doing just that.

'Just let it relax.'
And then the other thing:
if the water-drill were not
inside my mouth, I'd ask,
which of my many tongues
should I forget?
There are so many in here
and I fear they're not all mine,
not originally.

Before I come again, I decide
I must practise ignoring my
rebellious tongue,
forgetting it is there,
taking it out of combat.

Fragile afterwards,
on the ride back home
my smug tongue slides
like a happy slug
across a newly smoother tooth.

There's something to be said,
after all,
for giving in.

12 noon

Edges tattered, I have come
from miles away, crossed
borders, delivered my passport
distinguishing marks height
father's name date of birth
into the hands of many strangers
to reach this, a new country
peopled by shrill absences.

* * *

Here the light falls
heavily, pressing shadows
in where eyes should be,
lifting a cheekbone
burnt to white.

My eyes are in another hemisphere.
Behind the eyelids,
it is night.

* * *

Having got here,
what is there to say?
What can I do with this passport
anyway? It's just a means
to travel back and forth
between what is
and what might well have been.

And yet I still reach out
as if I were some old
blind lover, desperate
to seize and hold
and enter once again;

to press myself into this earth,
six feet or more.
Deeper, deeper.
All questions peeled away.

Crab-apples

My mother picked crab-apples
off the Glasgow apple trees
and pounded them with chillis
to change
her homesickness
into green chutney.

Front door

Wherever I have lived,
walking out of the front door
every morning
means crossing over
to a foreign country.

One language inside the house,
another out.
The food and clothes
and customs change.
The fingers on my hand turn
into forks.

I call it adaptation
when my tongue switches
from one grammar to another,
but the truth is I'm addicted now,
high on the rush
of daily displacement,
speeding to a different time zone,
heading into altered weather,
landing as another person.

Don't think I haven't noticed
you're on the same trip too.

Announcing the arrival...

The woman from Indian Airlines
stretches her voice languidly behind the ear.
'Announcing the Arrival of Flight 405,
another century, another year.'

Words arrive like terrorists
on this flight,
wedged in narrow seats
between tired businessmen
with bare forearms
and safari-suits.

Once thin boys,
stick figures tumbled from the sea,
cartwheeling on the beach,
all angles and bony knees,
they sliced the sky at Juhu, Mahim
Marine Drive,
in a frenzy of pure energy.

Grown to men who struggled
past a paunch to tie
their feet into shoes, this morning,
along with a Bombay dream or two.

And in some guest-house
late at night
after the chicken and rice
and pickle on the flight,
when they untie their shoe-laces
and free their swollen feet,
the stowaway words tumble out
hot from tarmac and city streets.

Announcing the Arrival....

Words circle above them, waiting.

Monsoon words

The best words come
like skilful monsoons.
They are the ones
that jump and bounce,
fall off the page
on to my mouth,
and cause singing.

If they're worth saying
they run distances, lift
themselves off pages,
and out of phones.
Your words are like that:
they have hands.

* * *

On the street, a man
counts eggs like gifts.
Someone laughs behind the wall.
A girl runs, sandal-flapping,
down the chattering road.
A child picks up a stone.
The stone opens one eye,
and blinks.

* * *

This madness is our main road.
Look away, and the rain will fall
on to your mouth.
The city's seashore drifts
a few words to the left.

We belong in this time,
after all.

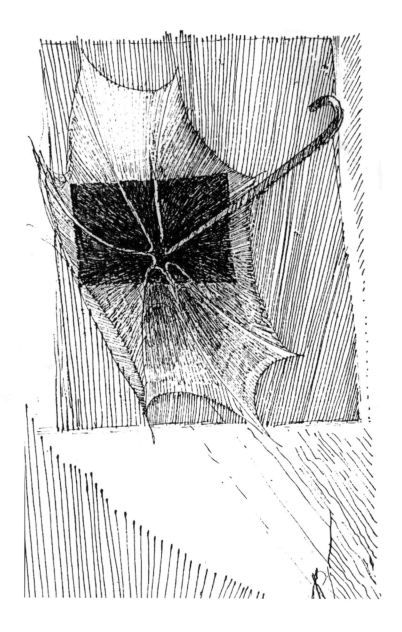

Announcing the arrival...

(for Ayesha)

It's time to face up to this.
The century was a bitch.
Thank god it's dead and gone
with its tail
between its legs
under a plastic tombstone.

Good riddance to bad rubbish
I say.
I was ready to junk it all
anyway,
throw it in a ditch,
the hypocrites, the prudes
running our lives
with their holier-than-thou prissy attitudes,
the bigots with offended sensibilities,
the bastards who'll put on
any party shoe that fits.
Who needs this shit?

At the end of every city street
I see the girl with flying hair,
who could be you,
scattered at the edges of my eyes.

So Ayesha,
let's put our faith elsewhere.
The new century is silvered
with those girls and you.
Let's paint our mouths and eyes
with opal, splash
iridescence on our breasts and thighs.

There is a potential in goodbyes.
This may not be freedom,
but it feels like wine.

Let's pretend the hand of a clock
moving forward by one second
can unhinge our lives.

The world shifts
with a lift of your hair.

Let's dance on the crazy rooftops
of Bombay.
Let's say
we're in love.
Let's scream
to the silent silverfish.
Let's admit we're mad,
let's wear red.

At the Lahore Karhai

It's a great day, Sunday,
when we pile into the car
and set off with a purpose –
a pilgrimage across the city,
to Wembley, the Lahore Karhai.
Lunch service has begun –
'No beer, we're Muslim' –
but the morning sun
squeezed into juice,
and 'Yaad na jaye'
on the two-in-one.

On the Grand Trunk Road
thundering across Punjab to Amritsar,
this would be a dhaba
where the truck-drivers pull in,
swearing and sweating,
full of lust for real food,
just like home.

Hauling our overloaded lives
the extra mile,
we're truckers of another kind,
looking hopefully (years away
from Sialkot and Chandigarh)
for the taste of our mothers'
hand in the cooking.

So we've arrived at this table:
the Lahore runaway;
the Sindhi refugee
with his beautiful wife
who prays each day to Krishna,
keeper of her kitchen and her life;
the Englishman too young
to be flavoured by the Raj;

the girls with silky hair,
wearing the confident air
of Bombay.

This winter, we have learnt
to wear our past
like summer clothes.

Yes, a great day.
A feast! We swoop
on a whole family of dishes.
The tarka dal is Auntie Hameeda
the karhai ghosht is Khala Ameena
the gajjar halva is Appa Rasheeda.

The warm naan is you.

My hand stops half-way to my mouth.
The Sunday light has locked
on all of us:
the owner's smiling son,
the cook at the hot kebabs,
Kartar, Rohini, Robert,
Ayesha, Sangam, I,
bound together by the bread we break,
sharing out our continent.

These
are ways of remembering.

Other days, we may prefer
Chinese.

Hanging Gardens

For quite a few years,
living next to the Tower of Silence,
my nearest neighbours were
the recent Parsi dead.

We grew close, as neighbours do.
Evenings, watching television
or taking my late walk,
I often thought of them
pale bodies offered to the elements,
Rumi, Boman, Hormusji, Shirin

waiting to be stripped
by the patient vultures.

And going out, I have always
expected from the sky
the falling finger, the forsaken toe,

the abandoned head,
the knowing, twinkling eye.

Not a muslim burial

Afterwards, I prefer you burn
my body,
rather than present it
plated up for worms.
While you're at it, burn my words,
and mix together all the ashes,
hand and page and face
ink and ankle-bone,
reduced to grey.

Scatter them in some country
I have never visited.
Or better still,
leave them on a train,
travelling
between.

No one must claim me.
On the journey I will need
no name, no nationality.
Let them label the remains
Lost Property.

They'll say, 'She must be from another country'

When I can't comprehend
why they're burning books
or slashing paintings,
when they can't bear to look
at god's own nakedness,
when they ban the film
and gut the seats to stop the play
and I ask why
they just smile and say,
'She must be
from another country.'

When I speak on the phone
and the vowel sounds are off
when the consonants are hard
and they should be soft,
they'll catch on at once
they'll pin it down
they'll explain it right away
to their own satisfaction,
they'll cluck their tongues
and say,
'She must be
from another country.'

When my mouth goes up
instead of down,
when I wear a tablecloth
to go to town,
when they suspect I'm black
or hear I'm gay
they won't be surprised,
they'll purse their lips
and say,
'She must be
from another country.'

When I eat up the olives
and spit out the pits
when I yawn at the opera
in the tragic bits
when I pee in the vineyard
as if it were Bombay,
flaunting my bare ass
covering my face
laughing through my hands
they'll turn away,
shake their heads quite sadly,
'She doesn't know any better,'
they'll say,
'She must be
from another country.'

Maybe there is a country
where all of us live,
all of us freaks
who aren't able to give
our loyalty to fat old fools,
the crooks and thugs
who wear the uniform
that gives them the right
to wave a flag,
puff out their chests,
put their feet on our necks,
and break their own rules.

But from where we are
it doesn't look like a country,
it's more like the cracks
that grow between borders
behind their backs.
That's where I live.
And I'll be happy to say,
'I never learned your customs.
I don't remember your language
or know your ways.
I must be
from another country.'

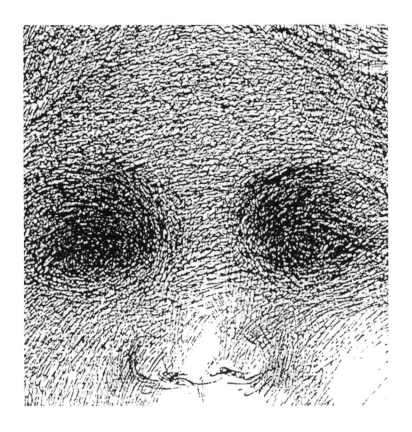

The broken umbrella

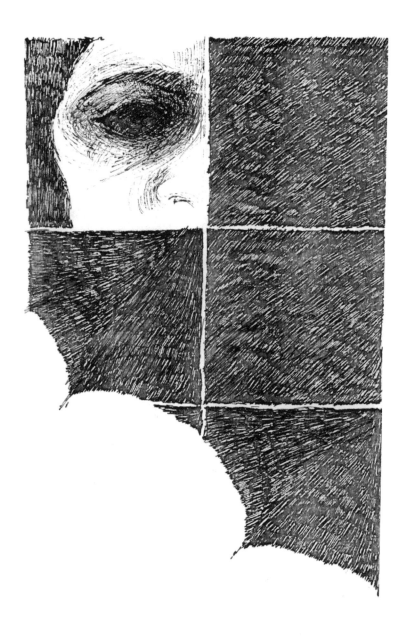

The umbrella

Somewhere in all the currency
of daily living,
getting, giving, squandering,
carelessly,
as if it were an old umbrella,
I lost your soul.

Ever since, I've looked out for it
in unlikely places, at the windows
of journeys I have never made,
among the angled bodies
of men on trains, rapt in papers
that save them
from a sunset or sunrise;
in airport lounges, in waiting rooms,
at stalls where people stand,
drinking tea,
in many queues, in spilt wine.

Somewhere in all the travelling,
conveyor-belts, check-in, security,
immigration, customs, duty-free,
I found pain.

I brush past strangers and look away.
Things have shifted.
My eyes lock on empty spaces.
I get out my boarding-pass.
I have forgotten where I want to go.

At Chowpatty, a woman is standing
under a crippled umbrella,
staring out to sea.

If I can't feel the rain,
she can't be me.

Outside

Halogen chills the street.
Lone men and women
hurry by, their collars pulled high
against the backlit sleet.
In the bright rectangle of a window
is a chair, a hollowed cushion,
a coffee-cup.

Sometimes (a trick of light,
a turn of the head)
you think you know that passerby.

I saw you at the kabootarkhana;
at Camden Market, from a bridge;
running down the Spanish steps.

Somewhere (in the night,
it's easy to make a mistake)
a bridge lifts, arches it's back
into the sky.

You know with certainty
(as I pass you
at a street-corner,
a turning in the stair)
that the one you are waiting for
never can be there.

Keeping guard

That dawn, the sky
arrived ablaze with light
shredded with seagulls' cries,
struck to stillness
with the force of flight.

It must have been
like any other day,
like all the ones I missed
by being in the wrong place;
like all the ones you missed
because you were asleep;

Each keeping guard over some
part of our separate skies.

Remind me not to look
when you open your eyes.

There is always the threat
of that delicate, dangerous dawn,
light-slashed,
wing-torn.

Remind me,
next time I go there,
to be alone.

In a cold place

My glove is sitting right here
on the table
with no hand inside.

The fingers are curled
as if they'd tried to grab
a fistful of air, then gave up,
realising the actual hand
had lost interest, and gone
elsewhere.

Leather wrinkles at the joints,
palm flat, not rounded
as it would be
with a juicy mount of Venus
tucked inside.

My hand is busy, writing,
stirring, dialling.
My hand picks up a steaming cup.

Beside it, my glove is waiting
for our needs to coincide,
for the moment when
its warm mouth,
my cold fingers
will happily, collide.

Today we spoke

I needn't have stroked your face.
We knew each other
before fingers.

It could go away quite easily.
Another day you will look at me
and see a wall.

Knowing doesn't make
a straight line.
Another day I'll call
and your voice
will shut the door politely.

There are no guarantees.

Today we woke
in separate countries
to different birds.
Yours sing, mine croak.

Today I broke
a silence.
You cut the blindfolds off my words.

Dot

This dot is standing here
quite still.
It is doing nothing
(or perhaps not).
It is a moment
poised in time
(not long).
It is movement
shifting into line.

Line that is word, bird.
Between my fingers, wings
explode into promises,
the knowledge that things
can break out
of their outlines,
shake off their shapes
to become other,
rare.
Turn into empty air,
catch at light,
trap shade
on the delicate edge
of danger.

I place myself here.
One dot. Hung
on the rush
of the earth's spin.
Colours burn.
Tastes explode on my tongue
like being born.
Textures jump to meet
my fingertips.
My outer layers swept away,
cloth strokes skin.
There is no way
to rein this pleasure in.

In the throat,
sound halts. And begins.
One seed of silence
ripens to a note of music.

We have found the voice
we share. Light soars
into arias.
When did this dot
learn to sing?

* * *

Hold your breath.
Touch my mouth,
and understand:
that words are doors
and dreams are floors,
and the walls we built
to hold the world
are only made
of light and shade,
a spinning space
where everything can change
again, and shift
with one lift
of your hand.

Knees

You can't take anything
for granted these days.

This bed is a boy
with knobbles for knees.
And I love you of course
but who knows how long?

Even potatoes sprout
unforeseen tusk and trunk
and we fall down
in ready adoration.

So don't shake anything inside my head.
Everything has its place
and I don't want it disturbed,
not even to be dusted,
do you understand?

Oh oh oh oh.
That was OK. Maybe
there's something to be said
for ignoring some of what I say.
Nothing's broken.
I just feel a bit
more rounded, suddenly.

The sofa cups its hands
and puts your fingers quite worshipfully
round my bottom while I watch TV.
This is nice. It doesn't take much
to make me happy.

I could live like this,
in deep belief,
indefinitely.

Sofa

Call it entanglement:
knees held under armpits,
ankles at the neck,
waist clamped between thighs.

No whys, no explanation
for how two bodies came
to be like this.

I give up all resistance
to sofas,

lost in the grip
of your sentences,
given away
to your unexpected movement,
your sly stillnesses.

Chair

There
in the half-light
between secrets and leaving
your shirt lies over my blouse
both tossed across the chair.

Fold laps at fold
shadows lick at light.
White and weave surrender themselves
more completely
than we would ever dare.

The cloth has learned to hold
the shape of breath between us,
shuffling the air
into knowing.

A give, a shift,
a share.

Yellow today

I am busy with making dreams
for the daylight to eat
when it gets up.

Orange and egg-yellow
splash up to the surface, ready
to be swallowed

whole.

Out of a ravenous night
and greedy sleep, I wake,
craving yellow things.
Spread the butter thicker.
Drizzle the day with honey.

This hunger is shouting for attention.
It wants your soul.

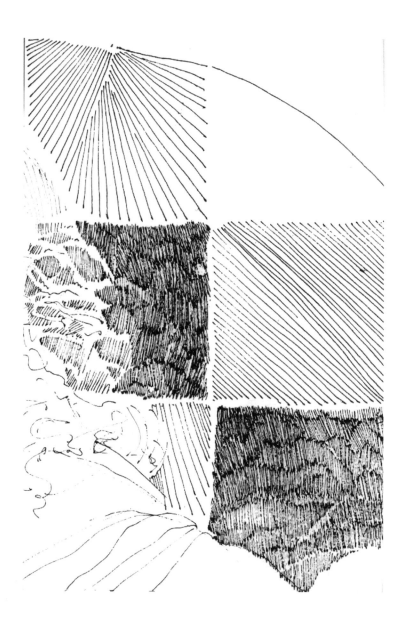

I speak for the devil

The djinn in Auntie

(for Ayub Khan-Din)

One minute she was out there,
screaming and cartwheeling
with the village boys,
slicing sunlight with bony legs
and high-pitched noise.

The next they said she must sit still
and shut her mouth.
She did it for a while,
right through a marriage and a child.

But one night when she went down
to the khassi, in the middle of her business,
that was when the djinn got in.
She didn't suspect a thing.

It took her by surprise, next day,
when she opened her mouth
and the other voice began to sing:
a sound, not hers.

And then the women and men came in
to hear her from miles around,
from villages she had never been to
or imagined,
asking her about people she had never seen.

Auntie on the bed
looked bigger every day, awash
with knowledge.
Crowds and questions filled the room.

Would Allah Rakha's son
make it to Dubai, and send back cash?
Would Bakka's lost child be found?
Would Barkat Ali's daughter be married soon?

The djinn worked the room.
The djinn knew all of them, knew just what to say
and answered everything, telling the truth
as far as anyone could tell –
up to a point of course:
No one asked if the groom
was gay.

In the morning, oiling the children's hair,
tying their red ribbons,
Auntie would always say,
'Don't stay too long in the khassi.
Watch out for the djinn.'

But secretly she knew
she'd be lost without the thing inside her.

Her djinn was a gift
she got one day
when she hoped for nothing.

Sometimes she feels as if her skin
has turned neon;
sometimes as if it's been
sewn it on a little tight.

And she's listening.
The djinn is whispering in there.
In another country, says the djinn,
that boy Ayub Khan-Din is drinking wine
and telling our story
to a woman in a skin-tight skirt
that shows all of her legs.

Her mother came from Mirpur,
just like us.
This woman has our look.
Set free, at last.

At last, possessed.

All of us

Rehmat Ali's wife sat down
quietly and said
someone else had opened up
her head.

Raju's mother started laughing
and they had to call the Brahmin in.

Ayub Khan's auntie went to the khassi,
met her djinn,
and started to speak in foreign tongues.

Mala killed a chicken and cooked it
with all the feathers on.

Naseem set fire to the bed,
and promised next time
he'd be in it.

Mary ran naked down the street.
Someone threw a sheet over her.

Anita never spoke back
to her mother-in-law,
but one day the devil did.

Sarah put slugs
in the cooking-pot
and waited for her bridegroom
to arrive.

Fatima was buried alive
and crawled out next day.

Dhamyanti was sitting under a tree
when the spirit swallowed her soul
like a sparrow.

This is a narrow road,
but we are on it,
more of us every day,
shouting out loud to one another
as if we'd met before, somewhere
on the way.

They can say we're out of control.
They can say we've gone
to the devil.

We are able to hear each other
now, laughing, screaming,
singing
with one mouth.

Power

SUJATA:

I bathed every day
took the flowers and went
to say hello to god.

The other side of god
was you.

Sometimes while I was feeding god
I smiled at you;
god knew.

One day I blinked
and fell into your mouth.

My own power swallowed me.

Time passed differently.
My heartbeat changed rhythm.
I started speaking to stones
and watched their mouths
when they spoke back to me.

Trees and rivers rearranged
themselves around my life.
Children came to touch my hands,
birds shook their wings out
in my hair.

My home became a person,
shifting to accommodate
what I had become.
I am the measure.
I have been moving things
to my scale.

They all walk around me
more carefully.
For the first time,
they look at me and see
more than clothes.

After a while they gave up
the electric shocks,
stopped the bloodletting,
realised there was nothing
to be gained by burning
hot coals on my skin.

It would take more than that
to make me give you up.

I close my mouth,
to keep the freedom in.

Breeding ground, Chicago

CHRISTINE:

I always knew I was carrying around
a breeding-ground
for the devil.

I mastered the art of nodding, smirking,
doing my hair just so
and wearing pink

to mask the stink of evil
lurking right inside my pride.

I could take the cleverest devil
for a ride.

A good thief cuts the glass
quite cleanly, without a noise
and enters.

There's hardly any sign
that things have been disturbed.

That's how the devil got in,
slipped into my skin,
rearranged my thoughts
like old clothes at the change
of the season.

Slice off my fingertips.
I mustn't leave our prints.

I'm burgling myself, and I'm so good
I won't be caught.

There's nothing here I'm afraid to lose.
Room after room of dusty corners
and mouldy shoes.

But what the hell –
Where are all the precious things,
the gold I thought I had,
the soul begging to be sold?

Learning to speak in Birmingham

ELLA:

I can't stand it. His breath is really bad.
He looked OK to start with,
maybe a little scruffy, fingernails bitten down,
someone who needed
looking after, a bit sad.
It wasn't as if he came looking for me,
not specifically.
He seemed to be busy
at the Bullring,
minding his own business.
I was minding mine,
wanting to be left alone as usual,
thinking my own thoughts.
My mind wasn't idle, no,
I wouldn't say so.
But I did look up and register
the abstracted look, the face of someone
flicking through a boring book.

And then he stopped, took notice
for one luminous second, focussed
on me.

One thing led to another.
We walked together.
He was odd: when I talked
he seemed to listen.

And suddenly the talking stopped.
One moment I could hear the sound
of my own voice.
The next I found
his breath inside my mouth.

It just took over.
I can still speak. There's no slurring.
My voice sounds different now.
The words are spilling off two tongues,
all flat and trite.

This is not the way
I thought it would be.
Maybe I struck a bad bargain,
imagined the taste of poetry.

But when you need something enough
you can overlook some faults.

And give him time.
He'll change.

Being good in Glasgow

FARIDA:

I did it all: read the Koran
five times at the seamen's club
that masqueraded as a mosque on Sundays,
kept the rosas,
fasted from dawn right through
the endless Scottish dusk,
 definitely never drank. Ate
fish and chips when all my
friends had hamburgers. If
I even thought of a pig I'd
spit.

I was really full of shit.

I got fed up with being good.
It must have been a put-on anyway,
because I was hungry to be bad,
like craving food.

What I wanted, really, deep down, was sin.
To open the front door
in the middle of the morning
and let the devil in.

Chilli-hot

There's a silence between us.
That's dangerous.
It could stretch into a crack
that lets the music in.

Here I am with my tongue
in your mouth.
Do you like it in there?
Do you like the sound it makes
when you whisper, softly, with my voice,
your own name?

* * *

Watch out.
I'm ready to love you
like the grinding-stone
loves the grain.

I'm about to love you
like the pestle pounding
green chillies
into chutneyed pain.

When I'm done loving you,
you'll be concentrated,
completely changed.

Ready or not,
here I come.

'Have you ever lost control?'

you asked, and passed the wine.
'Ever?'
    Every day the struggle
    to put one foot in front of another
    like other people do,
    to look like other people,
    pretending to be as sane
    as you;
    to act as if my brain
    doesn't dive dangerously
    off bridges and into
    other people's skins
    to behave as if I'm not guilty
    of all our secret sins.

    I walk around, I almost say,
    tuned to the inside of things,
    hearing everyone else's thoughts,
    feeling the boots rubbing
    on their feet,
    feeling their hearts
    beating in their chests.

    Only children give me space
    to breathe.
    Inside the small rib-cage,
    they are still unmoored
    and the sound of growing
    is a kind of rest.

    But if I don't hold myself
    quite tight
    it's too easy
    to step out of bounds,

    and then you'd know
    the crazy paving in my head,
    the cracks I can't walk on
    or else we're dead.

'Ever? Control?
No, I don't think so.
Maybe once, but that
was long ago.
I've forgotten now.'

I have myself in check,
hand clamped at the wrist,
my knuckles white.

My finger doesn't dip
into the wine.
The wine doesn't reach your mouth.

Maybe it will be all right.

Lines of control

If you wanted to start a fight
couldn't you just have got on with it,
the two of you, god and the devil
in deadly combat
tearing at each other
like cats in an alley;

but of all the battlegrounds
you could have chosen
why did you pick on me?

The eyelid trembles

Washing in and out of silence
in the moment before
it is gone; before
the bucket handle clangs
and the bolt is drawn,
before metallic water splashes
into the aluminium dawn,

in my dream I drink
from carefully cupped hands.
Someone pours
the water out for me.

I am the one who drinks
and the one who pours,
sliding in and out of my skin,
half myself, half someone else.

In the still space
before morning
the eyelid trembles.
There is only this
one membrane between us:
the one I am in sleep,
the thing I wake to be.

The location

The devil is real.
Power exists.
You can smell it feel it touch it
between the items on
your shopping-lists.

       *   *   *

I realised quite soon
the devil wasn't in the footsteps
echoing behind,

a sound that, when I looked back,
slid away, no body attached.

The devil was in me,
walking in my feet,
living in my clothes,
owning one half
of my heartbeat

       *   *   *

The devil never paid a penny for me,
he got me free,
just came and squatted
with no papers of occupancy,
no by-your-leave.

There was no buying, selling, bartering,
no attempt to deceive.
One day I felt occupied.
That was all.

In

A bit like morning sickness,
a djinn is something
you get used to.

When it's outside,
you can wave and call out its name,
wish it good morning,
Eid Mubarak
Have a Nice Day
Merry Christmas
Happy Diwali
as if it were a neighbour.

When it's in
it wears my name.
It shines inside my skin.
It anticipates the soft of baby hair,
loses its finger in the fat
behind the knees,
smells the baby powder there.
It lets me taste, in my mouth,
the secret burst of tamarind.

Like an angel, open my wings
and hear us, the first cry
the first note
blessed

begin

Close-circuit

You only get a glimpse:
a hand disappears around a door,
a mouth twitches off the mirror rim,
feet edge off reflecting surfaces,
the top of the head
is caught dead-centre
on the close-circuit camera.

Hard to say, right or wrong,
god or the devil,
with a ski-mask pulled on
casually over their purposes.

I put on different pairs
of glasses, to give me
alternative views:
one close, clear, sharp as nails,
one at a distance, set askew.

Matter is wavy, spread out in space.
Nature is a game of chance.
On the question of uncertainty
my mind takes dolphin leaps
from cunning skill to grace.
All truths fall away
like dodgy mirrors.

These are times
of strange alliances.

Satan, Saviour.
One of them was here.
Probability Rules, OK?

The devil's day

The other bastard's had his say.
Now it's my turn.
Give me half a chance
and you'll see things my way.

Try to understand my point of view.
You'll find it's not so strange,
quite familiar to you.

You think I'm burning
in some hell-hole?
That would be too easy.
I'll tell you what it's like.
It's like knowing you must have
something you can't have,
something that's not yours.

It's the ribbon of greed,
wanting to eat the food he eats
the small seed
of love in the wrong place.

It's seeing his face.
Wishing it were mine.

It's being hungry for his grace.

In bed with the devil

He's at it again,
making pacts for power,
hoping for a shower of goodies
if he plays it right.

He's spoken to the journalists,
shaken all the hands
smiled into the camera,
shown the proper sympathy; given gifts,
watched the briefcase
make it's way to inner rooms.

Secure at last
we can begin.

Saviours

It's hard to say
who's on which side.
All the murderers are wearing
masks
with god's face painted on.

The defenders of the faith
are devoutly contemplating
currency,
the slide of the rupee,
tumbling stock,
the taxi drivers' strike,
and whether
our Saviour will return
as a computer chip.

The price of onions has gone up:
the men around the table
decide it is appropriate
to go to war.

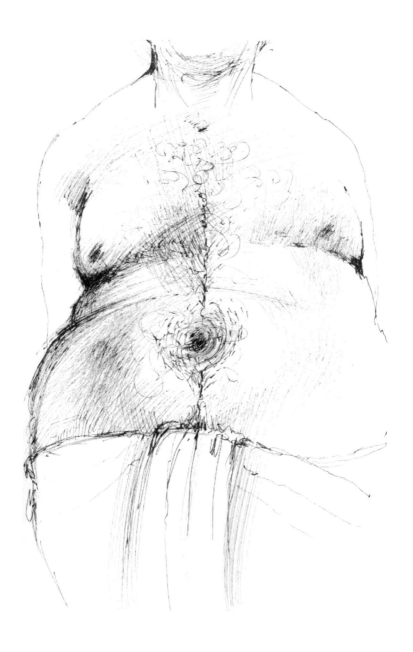

The devil to the poet

Don't pretend that you're
above all this.

When it comes to survival,
all your pretty words
and delicate observations
boil right down

to politics

Slit

Men have a rare genius
for revenge.

Spare me,
I don't know how the system works.

A car screeches
four thousand miles away.

It slits my skin.

* * *

Close by, a plane
explodes,
a sweetly offered garland
blows off someone's head.

I wasn't the one
who did this.

Ask the men carrying
holy books.

Ask god.
he knows.

Mobile

I've come to ask...
Don't answer if you can't.

It's just that in carriages overturned
spread across the railway track
the mobile phones have started
ringing.
No hand moves towards them.
No mouth turns to answer.
No one speaks.
No one says, 'Five minutes – I'll be there.'

The carriage windows are topside down.
Glass tears are falling upward
at you

forming questions, just begun.

I needed to know...
People must ask you these things
all the time.

This room

This room is breaking out
of itself, cracking through
its own walls
in search of space, light,
empty air.

The bed is lifting out of
its nightmares.
From dark corners, chairs
are rising up to crash through clouds.

This is the time and place
to be alive:
when the daily furniture of our lives
stirs, when the improbable arrives.
Pots and pans bang together
in celebration, clang
past the crowd of garlic, onions, spices,
fly by the ceiling fan.
No one is looking for the door.

In all this excitement
I'm wondering where
I've left my feet, and why

my hands are outside, clapping.

Guardians

Strange how the guardians
of our morals
have jellyfish mouths
and jamun eyes.

Funny how your fingers
slither into juicy things
where they don't belong;

how the pot-belly
sits with your holy abstinence.

Odd how, in those frequent mirrors,
your haloes don't show up,
and your media-buttered goodness
turns gargoyle.

In your face

In the face of adulterated gods,
in the face of easy betrayal,
in the face of your indifference

I have assembled
the rough materials to make
my own salvation,
collected secrets from non-resident spies
scattered across continents,
stockpiled laughter.

My finger is on the button.
I'm flying in your face,
trailing flame-ribbons
that will explode
your clay sky with questions.

Look.
I'm playing
with thin air and
through my fingers, wings swim
like riverhair.

Watch.
I'm a missile
falling upward.

Ceilings

I've been sleeping with the bats.
There's comfort in it, a snuffling
that's close to babies.

This morning the smell
swept me out. Hanging
upside down had numbed my feet.
The blood had rushed to the tips
of my ears and wings.

Tethered too long to clouds,
I need to cut free, perhaps
to some city on the bay
where every day spins on the edge
of danger, and they tie their buildings
down with sticks and strings
in case they fly away.

Flying is a bore. I'd rather fall,
I'd rather headfirst it through
the singing air to meet the kiss of heat,
burning sheets of paper, ideas
set on fire till all that's left
of them is blackened wings

that drift upward,
find ceilings,
and sighing like well-fed babies
fold into the crowdfall
of this
downward
sleep.

Mischief-maker

Oh Shaitan, Oh mischief-maker,
when I think I have you fixed,
imagining you are walking
in front of me,

I turn my head
and find you unexpectedly

behind, smiling with your eyes.

Remote control

I switch on the television set.
It flickers to life,
called up from another plane,

    moans,
    takes on tongues,
    tongues of angels,
    tongues of devils,
    tongues of men,

I have the power.
My finger shuffles life
and death. Chooses,
cancels, recalls –
a random strobe
that makes walls jump in and out,
    chairs dance,
    the floor yawn open
    the ceiling come back
    for more.

I wasn't looking for strange paths
to take.
They just were there,
appeared when I was unaware,

The others never knew.
They had their battles to fight,

dancing with their own devils
through the breathless night.

Dealing with the devil

Arshad said his uncle from Bradford
switched off the TV set one day
right in front of the children's faces
in the middle of Ice T,
dragged it out, smashed the screen
and carted the corpse away
to the dump,

leaving them sitting there,
the world cast out, all chatter exorcised,
Arif, Zubeida, open-mouthed Nasreen,
their faces left quite bare
as if they'd been pulled off.

One devil had been dealt with.
You have to start somewhere,
Arshad's uncle said.

Bai settles down

Bai settles down to MTV.
She could watch the Mahabharat,
vintage films: Amar, Akbar, Anthony,
vengeful gods or villains,
jiggling heroines – Sridevi, Madhuri.

But given the choice
and charge of the remote control,
after the cooking and washing's done,
this is what she wants to see:

A steamy scene involving garter-belts,
she giggles helplessly,
look at them eating each other's faces,
skinny scarecrows, rattling bones,
they could do with me
to cook for them.

She sees a naked pregnant woman.
Then, the image of the partner –
a pregnant man.

A long silence.
A battle happens on her face.
She searches through her life,
maybe looking for a point of reference.

At last, she formulates the question.

'Do all white men
have babies?'

A hope of justice somewhere in the world.

It brings the battle into your living-room

Of course, TV changes things.
You can stay right in the comfort of your native place
with the warm smells of chapatti and rice
coming out of your own kitchen,
carry on a conversation in your mother-tongue,
in Punjabi or Gujarati or Tamil.

While over there on your sideboard
strangers love and kiss and kill
spill the daily war across your dining-table
plastic faces bruised with battle,
bodies brutalised by careful knives
battered survivors from Miami, New York,
Beverly Hills.

The devil to god

Dear Sir,
I'm a fan of all your programmes,
but the promos are bad.
Who writes your scripts?
Can I apply?

Greater glory

I don't need temples
to glorify my name.
My house is your house,
your house is mine.

My work is in every
daily newpaper,
my word on every TV.

God was hijacked long ago,
held hostage in empty churches,
desecrated temples,
broken mosques.

Mine is the power and glory.
Mine is the audience.
Mine is the advertising.
Mine is the TRP.

Secrets

I will need to learn again
there is something I can't have.
A life that belongs
in another suitcase,
not mine.

Keeping secrets is the devil's work.
But who shall I tell my secrets to?

Shall I tell the other women?
Shall I tell you?

Telling it all is selling
your soul.

Give them knowledge,
and you're undone.
No one can get you back.
You're out in the abyss, alone.

So pack your hunger into
your own tin trunk,
hide it away.

Keeping secrets is the way
the devil finds to eat my heart.

A short detour from dying

Smash the mirror.
Smash the face that lives in there.
Watch it fly
out of uncertainty to madness,
catch the splinters in your eye.

You once had an image
of yourself,
simper in place,
all present and correct.

You once had an idea
of yourself.
Kiss it goodbye.

Canvas

Every day, I try to redraw my face.
I take a brush and crayons,
pens and pencils, paints and powdered
colours, and paint a face.

I paint it over the face I already have,
like a canvas I'd like to erase.

It's not that I don't like the face
god gave me,
but it looks unhappy,
the mouth turns down.

Over this, I paint another face
that smiles.
Then I rub it off. I don't want
a face that simpers harmlessly
like this.

Some day I plan to draw it
interesting, dangerous,

cruel.

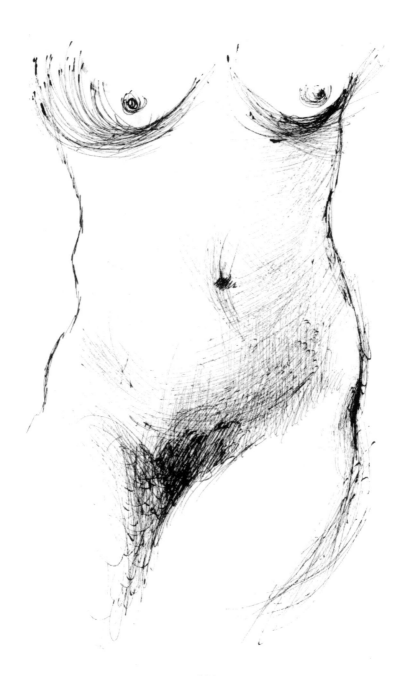

Compromising positions

Would it be more convenient
If we gave you a sack
Instead of a body? Maybe
a sack with a head?

There would be no temptation
then, to gratify it
dress it up, bare it
let it be misled.

Instead, it would be useful
to someone: filled, emptied out
refilled as required.
and the view from inside:
a loose weave of magic light.
At night, when there's no need of it,
it could be hung up;
or it could be left, without risk,
in bed.

No sweep of shoulder, shadowed rib
secret space at the hip-bone;
no hungers. A thing that never
clamours to be fed.

Except that the tongue is there,
It has needs, less to do with
hunger than with greed.
It says things that never should be said.

No, a sack with a head
and a tongue in the head
is still dangerous.

Leave the body on.
It doesn't really suit you but
it will have to do
until we can find something
more appropriate for you.

As it stands, the thing
is quite distressing to the public,
moving in mysterious ways
flaunting its disgrace
through centuries, in stone and paint
in photographs, on video-tape...

Squalid curves
and hollows caught
like ancient mysteries in frames.

Smooth as worship on the mouth
A hope of god between the collar-bones
a taste of faith beyond the flesh.

Object

Desire can be a delicate thing,
or so the punishments
suggest.
Who needs as much as the naked
breast? Lust
is aroused by a wrist
revealed,
the hollow at the neck,
the ankle-bone
half-concealed.

The guardians of our need
patrol the streets, fired
with pure passion,
eager to find the flesh
unsealed, frantic
to mete out justice.

Oh delicious.
Exquisite pleasure, to punish
the object of our desire.

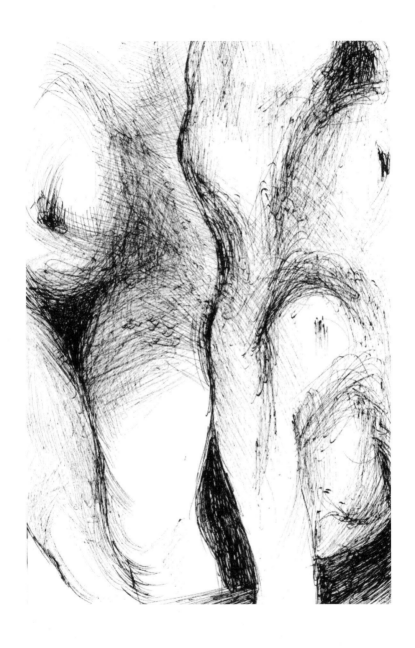

Medlar
(after a still life by Martius Nellius 1674-1706)

The painter began, they say,
with a pale ground,
then laid down the shadows
in dark brown, leaving the shape
of fruit intact.
It waited to be filled
with succulent colour, preparing
to be given highlights,
depths of weight and taste.

These medlars are ready
to be eaten only when
they show the first signs of decay.

Our deepest parts
are painted, sheer layer over layer
to let the light shine through.

In the tall glass.
the wine is glinting red,
underlit by our darkest need.

Delicious on the edge
of loss,
strange flesh sucked out
at the last moment,
at the very brink of waste.

Possession

The devil is a territory
that lets you believe you belong,
happy when you worship
at its mirrors.

The claws are on my shoulder,
breaking skin.
Hot breath in my ear.
This ground must be mine.
Pakistan, India, Kashmir.
Whisper the name of every place
I've ever been hatched in
or killed in.
In the end it comes
to the same thing.
The same bloody beak
and eyes.

Strange, the spies wear all the uniforms
of holy men and patriots, the saffron, green,
the smear of ash.

Meanwhile, our prayers
change from birds
to tigers outside this cage.

If you think this thing
sprouting demon wings
is planning to get off your back

you're wrong.

The devil's advice

The bigots have better
sound-bytes.

Shut up
and eat your food.

Prayer in the park

They're out with their socks off
and skirts up, shirtless,
letting the sun and air trampoline
on bouncy sheets of bare
pink, acres of backs and rolling buttocks,
toe-forests, himalayan ranges
of knees.

Oh please,
let not one cloud cross this
rollick of humanity.

For one more day
let the neighbours and their in-laws
drink white wine and Sprite
out of acrylic cups, let the children
waddle with duck-babies and
floppy pups splash with the swimmers
in the Serpentine.

(I'll pretend their peace is mine)

And let all the unwanted bits
of clothing rise up into the sky,
laughing and singing out loud,
link sleeves, lock trouser legs
and fly off across the adandoned city
sky divers in a maypole dance
around the OXO tower and the GPO.

Oh
let no shadow fall
on this happy day,
(this angelic crowd)

Blackbox

This sky hangs on the city
like old underwear
sagging at the belly and the bum.

These hands are dry fishes
left to wrinkle
in the sun.

The frame wobbles
from a hand-held camera.

'Gaddi aagaayi tation the,'

The train has come in at the station.
I am here to meet someone
who doesn't get off.

Songs make more sense to me
than holy books.

'Every day,' she said,
'I put on the prettiest knickers
in the world,
knowing that no one will ever see them
unless I fall out of a plane.'

That makes two of us.

When they make enquiries,
after the crash,
and open the black box of our lives,
what will they find?

A gasp. An exclamation.
An admiring silence.

Undressing

Don't be in too much of a hurry
to undress.
Let me do it for you, slowly.
Be patient –
I need to spend some time
at this collar-bone.
Bear with me while I get familiar
with this knee.

Forgive me.
My fingers are trying to remember
The texture of being free.

The devil's valentine

Through the night I wrote
notations on your skin,
whole letters on your shoulders,
across your back
and down your spine.

You never saw them, or
wrote back on mine,
never found the bits of words I'd left
lodged in crevices,
tucked under your armpits

Before bathing, every morning,
I'd check myself
all over, hips, legs,
between the toes,
just in case.

Not a line from you, though.
Not a word.

Yes, I drank the wine

Today I'm free
to party with the djinn.
Today don't call me.
I won't be in.

Squatter: left shoulder

I think
all my problems would go away
if I didn't have this person
I don't know
squatting in my brain all day.

He's in there, when I'm at the café,
sipping out of the same cup
slurping it up,
enjoying the taste of coffee
as much as me.

He's there at my left shoulder
when I read, glittering at
the line of poetry,
greedy like someone
who's bought Park Lane in *Monopoly*.

He was there in Venice when I went
alone, singing arias with the gondoliers.
And when I peeled that orange
he got it in the eye.
I felt him blink.

He has eyes and hands
right through the day,
with suspicious skill at
unfastening a bra.

But mysteriously, at night
when I need him most –
like a showy magician, without a sound,
without the cymbal crash
or roll of drums,
as if they were just a satin tablecloth
his smile and tongue and feet and fingers –
he whips them all away.

Last House-Full Show

We're all here at New Eros
across from the commuting crowds,
at the Last House-Full Show,
everyone you know, and everyone
you wish you didn't know

jostling into the balcony
and the stalls, all
the heavenly hordes with their wings
rolled up, god up there
eating popcorn with the VIPs,
the devil squeezed
into the back row with
the bad girls and boys.

The last judgement won't be boring,
Oh no, not a documentary,
not black and white but your
mis-spent life in glorious technicolour,
90mm, dolby digital,
we'll hear every sound you made,
every breath, groan, the crash and roar
of blood and joy and,
we hope, sin,
slick cuts, the camera locking in
to tight, tight close-up,
dizzy away to action scenes,

Prime Ministers dancing on top
of trains, politicians stashing
notes in bedsheets, big
women in bullet-proof capes,
caught by crane and helicopter.
This is a cosmic pull-out,
sky's eye view
of you.

* * *

Outside, crowds
are begging for tickets,
breaking down doors.
And the black marketeers
are doing roaring business.
It's a riot out there,
every enemy you've ever known
clamouring to get in,
to see all you've done,
every bad word, every betrayal,
so they can ban you, burn you,
throw you out.
Maybe that's what judgement's all about.

But imagine the rush
if they love you. What if
something you've said should
break through the me
to we?

                    *   *   *

Your theme song is on,
they're singing along,
a huge hymn,
they've heard the cassettes
and put down good money
to buy your voice

La la la happy now, but
a King Kong hand
could crush us all,
cyclone, volcano, earthquake, flood,
seats matchsticked, silver screen
scrunched, twenty-foot faces
tinselled to nothing,
popcorn scattered in the mud.

By some miracle we're
still here, blessed
with samosas and crisps in row JJ,
while a cheer goes up in stalls.
They liked the look
of that nuclear test,

frightening the mice from under
the seats, sending them
screeching over our feet.

And you there Bubbles Kapoor
and Mrs Dimple, you two
were not alone at the Heavenly
Cold Ring Home,
drinking rose faloodas at separate
sides of the plastic flowers
when the whole hall can see,
underneath the table,
the acrobatics of your knees.

Next to god, the Governor's mobile
goes off. The doors are shut,
you can't get out
or leave the auditorium for security reasons.
The slush machine's closed down.

Music pounding to the pelvic thrusts,
we must be part of this.
Our nails are on, our lipstick's fixed,
now is all we have, bliss
is in the jiggling hips.

                    *   *   *

Harmless pleasures. It's not as if
we've done much wrong.
Usually nothing more
than looking the other way,
keeping quiet,
going along.

These are people
I'm not sure I want to know.
Then why do I, uninvited,
own their memories?
Why do I flashback their lives
feel homesick for their childhood,
sit in their sofas,
as if they were my own?

At the back,
the devil is planning
a terrorist attack,
thoughtful, popping
the bubbles in the bubblewrap.
Plap!

He'll take pomegranates and put them
in your pocket, oranges
with tangy skin, send
pineapples flowering, garland
you with bananas.
Under his fingers, this fruit
will sing.

* * *

No one waits to see the scroll
of credits, the names of the ones
who lit you, provided the wardrobe
and the shoes.
Soon enough they'll have their moment
of fame, their time will come
to star in a story of their own.

And they're still coming in
from every corner of the city
over the flyovers,
under the bridges,
to this picture-show,
the butter-fed boys with fish fingers
for hands, the women
with no faces, to see
if they can find the life
beyond their recent death.

A breath
begins and lifts, lifts
us off the balcony
into empty air, and there,
everywhere around us, among the feet,
the wings and floating popcorn,
fingers unclurl; god opens
the closed fist.

125

Exorcism

I have to tell you.
You're playing with fire.
You strike me like a match.
I dagger your dark
with a blade of white light.

I hope you know this might
be dangerous.

* * *

I'm letting all the bad things
fall away. I'm no one
but myself,
no one possesses me.
The breath coming in
and out of my body
is only mine.

I'm in control of this,
I'm doing fine.

You won't find me in Sialkot
being someone's daughter.
You won't find me in Lahore
being someone's sister.
You won't find me in Bombay
being someone's wife.
You won't find me in London
being someone's mother.
You won't find me in Glasgow
being someone's nightmare.
You won't find me in Delhi
being someone's devil.
You won't find me in Rome
being someone's fantasy.

And if you're wondering,
I'm up here, alone.

My feet may be cold
but my breath is warm.

* * *

If you're looking for me
I'll be dancing on cans
and champagne bottles rolling
round the street, flying my feet
over the rattle and clunk
where the drums thump thump.

We're taking a chunk
out of a new song,
on the move
swirling, falling.

This is how we belong.